CUISINE SRI LANKA

By

Lambert R. Abeyatunge

This book is dedicated to my mother, Lizzie, my father, Morren, my late brother, Newton, and to all others from whom I learnt the art of creative Sri-Lankan cooking.

PROLOGUE

Cuisine Sri Lanka by Lambert R. Abeyatunge brings to America the wonders of one of the world's truly great and heretofore little-known cuisines. Says the author: "This book gives a general idea of the type of food consumed in Sri Lanka. It can teach the average American housewife how to add a touch of curry flavor to any type of food consumed by her family on an everyday basis."

Included in this delightful compendium are, among other tantalizing recipes, Spiced Fried Fish, Spiced Shrimp with Potatoes, Vegetable Curries, Stuffed Eggplant, Pumpkin and Squash Curries, Spiced Roti, and Watalappan (Sri Lanka Pudding). This veritable cornucopia of mouth-watering and nourishing dishes will "add a unique aroma and flavor to the food that you consume and will get you off the boredom of cooking steaks and casseroles as such! Instead, it will add excitement to the time you spend in the kitchen. With the knowledge of the basics outlined in this book, you will be able to create delicious and unique recipes with the products that you use on a daily basis."

Highly recommended as a fascinating and exotic collection of recipes that will make you proud to serve family members and friends, *Cuisine Sri Lanka* deserves a place in every home.

SRI LANKA – THE RESPLENDENT ISLAND

Sri Lanka, formerly known as Ceylon, is situated about fifty miles off the southeast coast of India. It is an independent island which was under the British until 1948. The British introduced tea to Sri Lanka and theirs is considered the best tasting tea in the world. The island is 272 miles north to south in its greatest length and 137 miles across at its greatest width. The trees and flowers are tropical, somewhat similar to those found in Hawaii. Mangoes, papayas, guavas, avocados, plantains, pineapples, and passion fruits are some of the tropical fruits found in this beautiful island. Anthuriums and orchids are found in many varieties. The average temperature is about 90º. The climate is somewhat dry and humid except in the hilly areas where the average temperature is about 70º and the climate is cool and comfortable. The humidity is lower in the dry zone. Seventy percent of the 15 million population are Singhalese Buddhists, twenty-two percent are Indian and Ceylon Tamils who are mostly Hindus. The remaining population consists of Malayans, Eurasians and Europeans. Lately several Americans have settled down in Sri Lanka and some have changed their religion to Buddhist philosophy. More than fifty percent of the population speaks English which is their second language. Sri Lanka is famous for its precious and semi-precious gems. The staple food of Sri Lankan consists of rice and curry. Fresh fruits are eaten for desserts. Fruit juice made from mango, orange, pineapple, and the passion fruit are the favorite midday drinks. In the villages coconut water is consumed to combat the thirst created by the excessive sweating due to the hot sun.

YOU COULD COOK SRI-LANKAN MEALS TOO!

This little book is designed to add a unique aroma and flavor to the food that you consume and will get you off the boredom of cooking steaks and casseroles and such! Instead it will add excitement to the time you spend in the kitchen. With the knowledge of the basics outlined in this book you will be able to create delicious and unique recipes with the products that you use on a daily basis. If you don't get it right the first time...don't give up...try again.

GOOD LUCK!

EQUIVALENTS

3 tsp	1 tbsp		2 cups	1 qt.
4 tbsp	¼ cup		4 cups	1 pt.
5 ¼ tbsp.	$^1/_3$ cup		16 ozs.	1 lb.
8 tbsp	½ cup		32 ozs.	1 qt.
10 2/3 tbsp	$^2/_3$ cup		1 liquid oz	2 tbsp.
12 tbsp	¾ cup		8 liquid ozs	1 cup
16 tbsp	1 cup			

PREFACE

This book is directed towards improving your accomplishments as a cook by enhancing the flavor by the addition of certain spices to the food that you normally prepare. This would take the boredom out of cooking the food in the same way often and from eating the same type of food every day.

There are some similarities between the preparations made in India, Sri Lanka and the West Indies. However, there are some ingredients that are peculiar to Sri-Lankan cooking.

Meat, fish, vegetables, and yams prepared with spices are generally referred to as CURRIES. The spices used in making curries can be bought individually or as a composite powder and sometimes as a composite paste. Most supermarkets carry these. They can also be bought from certain Indian stores in most major cities.

Sir-Lankan cooking utilizes coconut oil for frying and coconut "milk" for tempering the curries. The milk helps to form gravy of varying thickness depending on the amount of coconut milk used. The milk can be made from fresh coconuts by removing the white succulent center, cutting it into pieces and grating it with water in a blender. The resultant mixture should then be strained to yield the milk. Please remember that coconuts are rich in CHOLESTEROL. As such, I would advise you to limit the use of this ingredient.

In the absence of coconut milk you may use regular cow's milk to make the gravy and to enhance the flavor. Indian cooking is sometimes done with YOGURT which is of a higher nutritious value. Sweetened grated coconut available at the supermarket is not suitable for preparing curries. The spices also have a medicinal value and are, therefore, used in Sri Lanka as a treatment for colds and bowel ailments. The excessive use of the spices is not advised as this would ruin the taste of the food and you may develop an aversion from then on! Special crockery is not essential for preparing curries although in Sri Lanka and India utensils made of dried and kilned earth are used. I would also alert you not to add GINGER ROOT or powder to preparations made of MANIOC, which is a tropical yam sometimes sold in the supermarkets, as the mixture has been found to be fatal on a few occasions.

RICE is an integral part of the Sri-Lankan meal. It can be prepared in various forms either alone or in combinations with vegetables, meats or shrimp. A typical balanced Sri-Lankan meal is made of :

RICE

ONE PREPARATION OF VEGETABLE

ONE PREPARATION OF MEAT and

SOMETIMES A PREPARATION OF YAM

Most people in Sri Lanka, however, cannot afford to eat meat unless they kill the animal themselves. Brown rice is of more nutritive value than white rice as the former contains more vitamins, especially the vitamin B group.

CONTENTS

CUISINE SRI LANKA

WHAT IS CURRY?

Sri Lankans as well as Indians and West Indians Utilize CURRY POWDER in preparations made with meats, vegetables and yams. Curry powder is not a single ingredient but a mixture of spices and herbs which has been warmed or fried and blended in certain proportions. In Sri Lanka the ingredients are ground together on a wide flat stone using a rolling-pin shaped stone to grind the spices and herbs to a fine powder. The same can be achieved using a mortar and pestle or an electric blender. Commercially available curry powder is not made from the best spices and may have been adulterated with a certain amount of flour. To get the best taste and smell it is best to use the individual spices and grind them fresh as required. Storage causes some of the aroma and the taste to be lost. I shall try to outline some of the spices commonly used in Sri Lanka. Some of these may not be available from your supermarket. An address is provided at the end of the book in the event you would like to MAIL ORDER good quality curry powder from SRI LANKA.

SOME COMMONLY USED SPICES AND HERBS

CHILLIES

This is a fruit containing mild to very "hot" seeds enclosed in a juicy capsule. The shrub is a native of South America. The Portuguese carried the seeds to India and Sri Lanka and later spread throughout the Orient. The smaller green chilies are generally "hotter" than the larger juicy peppers. In general cayenne pepper is made from hot pepper. Green chili peppers vary in size from about one-quarter inch to five inches in length. In the recipes calling for one green pepper use one of about one to one-and-one-half inches in length. If you like a mildly "hot" curry remove the seeds from the chili pepper before adding it to the mixture.

ANISEED

This is a seed from a herbal plant found all over the world, but originated in the Mediterranean. It is used in breads, cakes, candies, and in certain liquors. Aniseed has some medicinal properties as well as acting as carminative.

ONION

Onion needs no introduction as it is commonly used throughout the world. However, there are certain onions that are peculiar to the tropical lands. These are smaller and have a distinctive taste when compared to the somewhat bland taste of the large onions which originated in India (sometimes called Bombay onions).

CARDAMOMS

These are the ripe fruits of a herbaceous plant native to Sri Lanka and certain parts of India. It is a major export of Sri Lanka. In ancient times these seeds were used as an aphrodisiac. The little black seeds inside the small fruits impart a very strong aromatic smell and taste to the food it is added to. The seeds should be left inside the fruit until ready to be used.

CINNAMON

The cinnamon tree grows to a height of about forty feet and is found exclusively in Sri Lanka and a few parts of India. It is one of the earliest known spices. The dried bark of the tree is used as a spice. It is again a major export of Sri Lanka.

CLOVES

Cloves are the dried unopened flower buds of the clove tree which is found in several tropical islands including Sri Lanka. The clove tree grows to a height of about thirty to forty feet, has shiny green leaves which have a very pleasant distinctive aroma. The flower buds are harvested several times a year and dried in the sun until they become brown.

CORIANDER

The coriander seed is derived from a herb. It is found in the Mediterranean, North India and in Sri Lanka. It was used as an aphrodisiac in ancient times. The leaves of the herbaceous plant are also used to garnish certain curries.

CUMIN

Cumin is derived from a small herbaceous plant. Though it originated in the Middle East, it is cultivated throughout the world.

GINGER

This is derived from the root of a small herbaceous shrub extensively used in the East as well as in Western cooking. It is available in the dried root, fresh root and powdered forms. Whenever possible the fresh ginger root should be used in order to get the best flavor.

MUSTARD

Mustard seeds have medicinal properties in addition to their culinary properties. There are two varieties, black and white. The seeds of the black mustard produce a more pungent volatile oil.

NUTMEG AND MACE

Nutmeg and mace are derived from the fruit of the nutmeg tree which grows in tropical climates. The commercially used nutmeg is derived from the seed and the mace from a network of red outgrowth which envelopes the seed. These are dried and powdered to make nutmeg and mace powder commercially used.

PEPPER

The black and white peppers are derived from the same tree. Black pepper is stronger and more aromatic than white pepper since the black skin imparts a certain amount of pungency.

SAFFRON

Saffron is derived from the dried stigmas of and styles of the flowers of the saffron tree. It is known to have certain medicinal properties in addition to the culinary properties. In Sri Lanka and in India it is also used as a die. However, the color fades with time.

Addition of saffron to curries and rice preparations imparts a slightly pleasantly bitter taste and a golden yellow color to the food.

TURMERIC

Turmeric is very similar to saffron in its properties and color but it is derived from an underground root similar to the ginger root. The root is brilliantly orange-red in color.

CURRY POWDER

Ingredients

½ cup coriander seeds.

½ cup ground turmeric.

1 dried red chili pepper.

1 tablespoonful of cloves.

1 ½ tablespoonful of ground ginger.

1 tablespoonful anise seeds.

1 tablespoonful ground mace

2 tablespoonful of cumin cinnamon.

1 ½ tablespoonful of ground red pepper.

1 tablespoonful of ground mace.

2 tablespoonful of cardamom seeds.

$^1/_3$ cup whole black pepper.

Preparation: Place the above ingredients in an electric blender. Process until the mixture is finely ground. Store in a jar and make sure the lid is closed tightly to prevent the aroma and the spicy taste from being lost. The amount of red chili added will determine how "hot"

the mixture is. Curry paste could be made by heating the above mixture in vegetable oil.

PREPARATIONS MADE FROM RICE

PLAIN RICE (BROWN OR WHITE)

Ingredients

Rice. One cup per person   ¼ teaspoon of salt.

1-3 teaspoonful of butter or margarine depending

on the amount of rice being cooked.

Preparation: Wash the rice several times until the white powdery coating has been removed. Add one cup of cold water for each cup of rice and two extra cups for the pot! Boil the mixture on medium heat and add the salt before all the water evaporates. Mix thoroughly and add the butter. Allow to simmer on low heat until the rice is soft. The mixture should not be "tacky". If tacky, next time reduce the amount of water added.   The rice is now ready for serving.

Variations: Rice can be cooked in special electrical rice cookers available from appliance stores for perfect results. The rice can be colored yellow by adding a "pinch" of TURMERIC. Raisins may be added to enhance the taste and to entice youngsters.

MILK RICE

Milk rice is consumed usually at breakfast time.

Ingredients

Rice, either brown or white.   ¼ teaspoon of salt.

1-3 cups of either coconut milk

or cow's milk.

Preparation: Wash the rice thoroughly and cook as for plain rice. When the rice is partially cooked, add the salt and the milk and cook until well done. The final result should be a tacky mixture of rice and milk. Spread the rice on a flat plate and allow to cool. Cut into squares and the milk rice is now ready for consumption.

FRIED RICE

Fried rice mixed with certain vegetables and shrimp, lobster, pork or beef will make a delicious meal all by itself. Preparation of shrimp fried rice is described in detail here. By substituting pork or beef for the shrimp the meal may be varied to one's own taste.

Ingredients:

Plain rice prepared as explained in an earlier section.

½ head of lettuce very thinly sliced.

2 carrots thinly sliced.

small head of cauliflower cut into small flowers.

2 eggs hard boiled and chopped into small pieces.

1 pound small shrimp cleaned, deveined and washed with lemon juice and water

4 tablespoons of oil.

1 teaspoon of salt.

1 tablespoon curry powder.

Preparation: Prepare plain rice and set aside. In a large frying pan or a WOK heat the oil. Add all the ingredients except the lettuce, shrimp and the eggs. Fry for about 3 minutes. Add rice and mix thoroughly. In a separate pan fry the shrimp and the shredded eggs until the former is well cooked. Add this mixture to the spiced rice mixture in the WOK or the larger pan. Mix thoroughly. Finally sprinkle the finely sliced lettuce over the fried rice after transferring to the serving plate. The addition of 3 cloves and 3 cardamoms will greatly enhance both the taste and the smell of fried rice.

Shrimp Fried Rice

MILK RICE WITH TREACLE OR HONEY

Ingredients

1 cup of treacle or honey.	1 mature coconut finely grated or sweet grated coconut.
25 cumin seeds.	Milk rice made as before.

Preparation: Heat the treacle or honey until it reaches a sticky consistency. Add finely grated coconut and the cumin seeds that have been roasted and powdered. Mix until the coconut becomes sticky. Place some of the milk rice prepared as in the previous recipe and flatten. Place some of the coconut mixture in the center and fold the rice over and "fuse" the margins. The folding may be facilitated by spreading the rice on aluminum wrapping paper or paper used for freezing food. This makes an excellent snack for an afternoon tea.

YELLOW RICE

Ingredients

Rice. 1 cup per person	4 ozs. of GHEE or butter.
6 Cloves.	Pinch of turmeric.
Pinch of salt.	Coconut.
Cardamoms. A few curry or bay leaves.	1 onion.

Preparation: Heat the butter or ghee with chopped onions, curry or bay leaves and fry until brown. Add washed rice and mix well. Dissolve the salt and the turmeric in coconut milk. Add the cardamoms and cloves. Bundle the latter ingredients in a piece of cloth. Add the bundle to the cooking rice and allow to boil. When the rice is par-boiled remove the bundle. Cook the rice until well done. Allow to simmer and serve.

CURRIED PREPARATIONS OF MEAT, FISH AND EGGS

MEAT CURRY

Any kind of meat (beef, lamb, venison, etc.) may be substituted in any of the following preparations. The curry may be made mildly spicy hot, moderately spicy hot or very spicy hot by altering the amount of hot pepper and curry powder added. It is advisable to start with a mildly spicy curry.

FISH, SHRIMP AND LOBSTER CURRY

The fishy odor of these could be eliminated by pouring a little lemon juice mixed with water, allowing to stand for a little while and then washing with fresh cold water.

EGG CURRY

Eggs should be hard boiled and peeled. It may be used as it is or covered with batter and fried before making the curry.

BEEF CURRY

Ingredients:

1 pounds of cubed beef or lamb or pork (remove the fatty and

EITHER 1 tablespoon of CURRY POWDER OR PASTE OR 2 tablespoonfuls of ligamentous tissue). ground coriander.

1 teaspoon of cumin. ½ teaspoon paprika.

½ teaspoon finely chopped ginger ¼ teaspoon cayenne pepper.

Pinch of ground cinnamon. 3 medium onions thinly sliced.

4 tablespoons of vegetable oil. 6 cloves of garlic, crushed.

1 ½ cups of water. 1 ½ teaspoons of salt.

½ cup of yogurt or milk.

Preparation: Mix the meat cubes and crushed garlic together and set aside for about 1 hour. Heat the vegetable oil and add in the sliced onions and fry until brown. Add the curry powder or the paste or the individual spices and fry for another 2 minutes. Put in the meat and fry for another 5 minutes. Add the water and let simmer. Add the salt and let the curry simmer until the meat is tender. Add the yogurt just before serving making sure the curry is mixed well with the yogurt or the milk as the case may be. By varying the amount of yogurt or milk used, the curry may be made to have a thick or a thin gravy. If you would like a real hot and spicy curry be sure to add a sliced green hot pepper.

FRIED MEAT CURRY

Tasty fried beef or lamb cubes will make a delicious side dish especially when enjoying a beer or any alcoholic beverage. The same ingredients are used.

Preparation: Mix the washed cubes of the meat with curry powder, paste or the individual spices which have been previously ground together in a mortar and pestle or with a kitchen mallet or rolling pin. Let the mixture stand for about 1 hour. Fry the onion slices in oil and add the cubes of meat and salt to taste.

Note: Do not add water, milk or yogurt as this would make gravy. Serve when the meat is fried and tender.

SPICED FRIED LIVER

Ingredients

1 teaspoon of turmeric.	1 teaspoon of grated ginger.
2 cloves of crushed	¼ teaspoon of cayenne

garlic.

pepper.

¼ teaspoon of black pepper.

1 tablespoon of vinegar.

1 pound liver.

3 tablespoonfuls of vegetable oil.

2 medium onions sliced thin.

Juice from ½ a lemon.

1 teaspoon of salt.

Preparation: Mix all the spices mentioned above in a mortar or in a pan. Wash and pat dry the liver which has been cut into cubes. Rub the cubes with the spices which should now be in the form of a paste. Heat the vegetable oil and fry the onions until golden brown. Put in the cubes of liver and fry until the cubes are brown and well cooked. Sprinkle with lemon juice and the salt before serving.

SPICY CHICKEN CURRY

Ingredients

2-2 ½ lbs. of choice chicken cut into pieces or disjointed. Personally I like to remove the skin before cooking but many cook with chicken parts dressed!

4 tablespoons of vegetable oil or clarified butter.	1 ½ teaspoons of mustard seeds warmed in a pan before crushing.
2 cloves of crushed garlic.	1 tablespoon of cardamom seeds.
1 teaspoon of cumin seeds.	1 tablespoon of ground coriander.
2 fresh green chilies finely chopped.	¼ teaspoon of finely chopped ginger.
1 teaspoon of turmeric.	1 teaspoon of salt.
1 cup of water.	1 cup of yogurt or coconut milk or cow's milk.

Preparations: Sauté onion and garlic in the oil until golden brown. Add the coriander, turmeric, cumin, mustard, ginger, and the chilies. Fry the mixture for several minutes. Add the chicken and sauté for 5 minutes. Add the salt and water. Cover and simmer for about 15 minutes. Stir in the yogurt or coconut milk or cow's milk and continue simmering uncovered until the chicken is very tender. Remove from heat and add about 2 tablespoons of lemon juice to enhance the taste before serving.

The total cooking time for this curry will be about 30-45 minutes depending on the amount of chicken used. Certain vegetables may be added (e.g.; spinach, cabbage) halfway through the process.

CURIED EGGS

Ingredients

Hard boiled eggs (8) each cut into quarters.	1 chopped onion
1 clove of crushed garlic.	2 teaspoons of curry powder or paste.
1 teaspoon of ginger, finely chopped.	½ teaspoon salt.
¼ teaspoon cinnamon.	Pinch of black pepper.
½ cup water.	2 cups milk.

Preparations: Heat oil in saucepan on medium heat. Add the onion, garlic and the ginger and fry until golden brown. Add the curry powder or the paste and mix thoroughly. Add the milk and mix until a thick gravy is formed. If necessary a few tablespoons of flour can be added to make a thicker gravy. Now add the quartered eggs. Sprinkle the salt, cinnamon and the black pepper. The curry is now ready to be served on rice.

SEA FOOD PREPARATIONS

Remember to soak fish, shrimps, lobster, clams, etc., in lemon juice and water before cooking in order to remove the "fishy" smell.

FISH CURRY

Ingredients

1 lb. fish cut into pieces.	1 bay leaf crumbled.
1 teaspoon salt.	¼ teaspoon mustard seed.
1 or 2 fresh hot green chilies finely sliced.	4 tablespoons vegetable oil.
2 medium onions, thinly sliced.	2 or 3 cloves.
1 tablespoon curry powder.	½ teaspoon grated ginger.
2 cups milk.	1 tablespoon white vinegar.

Preparation: Dry the pieces of fish between paper to remove water. Fry in a pan until golden brown. Set aside. Add the sliced onions to the pan and fry until brown. Add ginger, bay leaf, mustard, green chilies, curry and the cloves and fry for another 2 minutes. Add the fish and mix thoroughly and cook for about 2 minutes. Now add the milk and cook further for another 15 minutes. Stir in the vinegar and salt and let simmer before serving on rice.

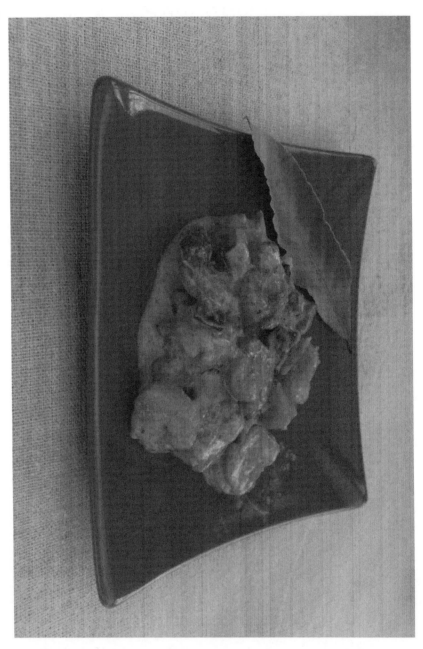

SPICED FRIED FISH

Ingredients

1 lb. fish cut into pieces.	1 teaspoon cumin.
1 teaspoon salt.	1 teaspoon cayenne pepper.
¼ teaspoon turmeric.	2 cloves garlic.
2 medium onions.	3 tablespoons vegetable oil.
1 teaspoon mustard seeds.	2 tablespoons water.

Preparation: Rub the fish with salt and turmeric and seaside. Chop one of the onions and mix with mustard seeds, cumin, cayenne pepper, and garlic in a food mill or an electric blender. Heat the oil in a pan. Fry the remaining onion which has been finely chopped until brown. Add in the fish and fry for several minutes. Now add the ground onion paste mix and stir into the fish until the latter is thoroughly coated with the mixture. Sprinkle in the water. Cover the pan and let the curry simmer until the fish is tender.

SHRIMP PREPARATIONS

Remember to remove the dark linear organ on the back of the shrimp (intestines containing sand).

SPICY SHRIMP CURRY

Ingredients

2 lbs. shelled and cleaned shrimp.

1 teaspoon salt.

1 teaspoon cumin powder.

2 tablespoons ground coriander.

2 cloves garlic.

1 teaspoon crushed red pepper.

4 tablespoons oil.

1 teaspoon turmeric.

Juice from 2 lemons.

2 tablespoons chopped chives.

Preparation: Mix the salt, red pepper, cumin, turmeric, garlic, and the coriander with the shrimp and let it stand for about an hour to marinate. Heat the oil in a pan and add in the shrimp mixture and cook until tender. Just before serving add lemon juice and the chives.

SPICED SHRIMP WITH POTATOES

Ingredients

2 lbs. shrimp

1 teaspoon cumin.

3 potatoes cut into cubes.

2 cloves of garlic.

6 tablespoon oil.

1 teaspoon salt.

½ teaspoon turmeric.

1 teaspoon chili powder.

2 fresh green chilies.

Preparation: Heat 3 tablespoons of oil and sauté potatoes until half done. Drain the oil and set aside. Combine shrimp, chili powder, garlic, turmeric, cumin and the salt. Add the remaining 3 tablespoons of oil and the shrimp to the pan. Sauté for several minutes. Add the potatoes and continue cooking until done. Serve garnished with chopped green chilies and you may add some fresh coriander leaves if available.

Note: Lobster and crab meat could be curried in the same manner with the same ingredients.

VEGETABLE CURRIES

Since a large number of Sri Lanka's population is vegetarians it is not surprising to find some of the most delicious dishes in that isle. Most tropical vegetables can be bought from large grocery chain store from time to time. These are imported from the West Indies and Hawaii. There are many ways to make your vegetables tasty by the addition of spices. Since vegetables are rich in vitamins (especially the leafy vegetables), make sure you do not over-boil or over-cook them. The following recipes are only a few of the most popular Sri-Lankan vegetable preparations which can transform a simple meal into a delightful taste-experience.

Some of the commonly used vegetables:

Eggplant (also called Brinjal)-
Okra
Kerala (Not easily available except in large cities)
Beans
Cabbage and Cauliflower
Spinach
Pumpkin
Squash
Potatoes, Sweet Potatoes

SPICY EGGPLANT CURRY

Ingredients

3 small eggplants.	½ cup coconut.
6 tablespoons oil.	Juice from 2 lemons.
1 tablespoon ground coriander	1 teaspoon salt.
1 teaspoon chili powder.	1 bay leaf.
¼ teaspoon turmeric.	1 fresh green chili (chopped).
3 large onions finely sliced.	1 teaspoon mustard seeds.
3 cloves crushed garlic.	1 teaspoon brown sugar.

Preparation: Cut the eggplant lengthwise into several segments. Fry in 4 tablespoons of the vegetable oil. Set aside. Fry the coriander, garlic, chili powder, green chili, and onions for about 5 minutes in the remaining oil. Add the grated coconut and fry for another 3 minutes. Put in the lemon juice, bay leaf, salt, a little water and stir well. Add the eggplant slices and cover the pot and let simmer until the eggplant is tender and the sauce is sufficiently thickened. Add the brown sugar and mustard which had been fired in a little oil until they pop. Mix well and serve on a plate of rice.

EGGPLANT CURRY

Ingredients

2 medium onions – chopped.	½ teaspoon chili powder.
4 tablespoons oil.	½ teaspoon turmeric.
3 cloves garlic.	1 large eggplant.
2 tablespoons green pepper - finely chopped.	½ teaspoon grated fresh ginger.
1 teaspoon salt.	3 large tomatoes – chopped.

Preparation: Sauté the onions until golden brown. Add the chili powder, turmeric, green pepper, garlic, and the ginger and fry for about 3 minutes. Cut the eggplant into small cubes and add it to the above mixture. Fry for another 10 minutes stirring constantly. Add a little warm water and simmer in low heat for another 10 minutes.

STUFFED EGGPLANT

Ingredients

½ cup vegetable oil.

1 teaspoon salt

2 tablespoons ground coriander.

1 bay leaf.

3 small eggplants.

2 teaspoons cumin.

1 teaspoon mustard seeds.

1 tablespoon lemon juice.

½ teaspoon chili powder.

1 teaspoon turmeric.

½ cup grated coconuts.

2 medium onions – thinly sliced.

1 cup of water.

.

Preparation: Heat about 2 tablespoons of the oil in a pan and add the cumin, coriander, turmeric, chili powder, and the grated coconuts and fry for a few minutes. Add lemon juice and salt. Slit the eggplant three quarters of the way through and stuff it with the above spiced coconut mixture. In another pan or a casserole dish, heat 2 tablespoons of oil and add the mustard seeds and fry until the seeds pop. Add the onions and fry until golden brown. Add the bay leaf and the rest of the spiced coconut mixture. Place the eggplant in the dish, add some water, cover and let it simmer until tender.

BEAN SPROUTS

Ingredients

2 tablespoons oil.

¼ teaspoon turmeric.

2 medium onions – chopped.

½ teaspoon ground ginger.

½ teaspoon cumin.

1 clove crushed garlic.

1 tablespoon grated coconut.

½ teaspoon salt.

1 lb. bean sprouts.

1 cup coconut milk.

Preparation: Sauté the onions sliced thin in oil until golden brown. Add cumin, coconut, ginger, turmeric, garlic, and salt. Fry for 2 to 3 minutes. Add bean sprouts and the coconut milk. Simmer for about 10 minutes. Serve with rice, bread or pita.

SPINACH AND POTATO CURRY

Ingredients

3 medium potatoes peeled and quartered.

4 tablespoons oil.

1 teaspoon grated ginger.

2 cloves crushed garlic.

¼ teaspoon cayenne pepper.

1 teaspoon salt.

1 lb. spinach – chopped.

Preparation: Heat vegetable and add the potato quarters. Cook until brown. Put in all the spices and fry for several minutes. Add spinach, cover pan and fry until the potatoes and spinach are tender.

CAULIFLOWER CURRY

Ingredients

1 teaspoon ginger.

3 tablespoons oil.

2 cloves crushed garlic.

1 teaspoon cumin.

1 teaspoon salt.

¼ teaspoon grounded cardamom.

¼ teaspoon black pepper.

$^1/_8$ teaspoon cinnamon.

1 cup yogurt.

$^1/_8$ teaspoon ground cloves.

1 medium cauliflower cut into pieces.

3 medium onions thinly sliced.

1 cup of water.

Preparation: Add the ginger, garlic, salt, and black pepper to the yogurt and mix thoroughly. Add this mixture to the cauliflower and mix again. Fry the onions in the oil until golden brown. Put in the cumin, cardamom, cinnamon, cloves and mix well. Fry for about 3 minutes. Add the cauliflower mixture to the spices and fry on low heat for several minutes. Add the cup of water and allow to simmer until the cauliflower is tender. You may add sliced tomatoes for added taste.

PUMPKIN OR SQUASH CURRY

Ingredients

1 pumpkin or squash cut into¼ inch squares.

1 ½ teaspoon salt.

2 tablespoons vegetable oil.

1 bay leaf.

1 teaspoon ground mustard.   1 sliced onion.

2 tablespoons grated   1 cup milk or yogurt. or
coconut.   paste.

1 tablespoon curry powder

Preparation: Heat the oil in a pan and add the sliced onion. Fry until golden brown. Add the curry powder or the paste and the ground mustard and fry for about 2 minutes. Now add the pumpkin or the squash and mix thoroughly. Add about a ¼ cup of water and allow to cook until the pumpkin is half done. Add salt and the grated coconut and mix well. Add the milk or the yogurt and the bay leaf. Cover and allow to cook in medium heat until the pumpkin is well done.

OKRA CURRY

Note: Okra may be purchased fresh or the frozen form. The latter is available in whole or cut into smaller pieces.

Ingredients

1 lb. okra.   1 teaspoon cumin.

½ teaspoon turmeric.

2 teaspoons ground coriander.

¼ teaspoon cayenne pepper.

1 teaspoon salt.

3 tablespoonfuls of vegetable oil.

Preparation: Slice the okra into small pieces and wash thoroughly until the slimy sap is removed. Heat oil and add the spices. Add the okra and cover. Allow to cook in medium heat and stir occasionally. Add the salt. Remove when the okra is tender.

STUFFED OKRA

Preparation: Wash whole okra and slit longitudinally halfway. Mix together the same spices as for the curry and stuff the okra with this mixture. Heat the oil in a pan and carefully place the okra in the pan. Sprinkle some lime juice and cover. Let the okra cook over low heat for about half an hour. Roll the okra to prevent them sticking to the pan.

LENTIL, DAHL AND CHICK-PEA CURRY

These are a good source of proteins. Lentil is usually available in packers of the grain with a greenish "skin." Dahl is found already "deskinned" in yellowish orange grain. Another grain that is very rich in proteins and consumed in Sri Lanka is the MUNG grain. This is found in the deskinned form and in pure form with a green skin.

LENTIL CURRY

Ingredients

1 cup lentils.

3 cloves chopped garlic.

1 medium onion, finely sliced.

1 teaspoon salt.

¼ teaspoon turmeric.

2 teaspoons coriander powder.

½ teaspoon red pepper.

3 tablespoons vegetable oil.

Preparation: Heat the vegetable oil in a pan and add the slices of onion and fry until brown. Add all the ingredients or substitute 1 teaspoon of curry powder or the paste and heat for another 3 minutes. The lentils should be presoaked for about 1 hour. Drain the water and add the lentils to the pan. Fry for another 5 minutes. Add 1 cup of water or coconut milk and turn down the heat to low. Cover the pan and cook for about 1 hour. Add the salt and mix well. Serve with rice.

MUNG DAHL CURRY

Ingredients

1 cup whole mung dahl soaked for 1 hour.

1 grated onion.

¼ teaspoon turmeric.

1 onion thinly sliced.

¼ cup grated coconut.

¼ teaspoon cumin.

2 fresh green chilies finely chopped.

1 teaspoon salt.

Preparation: Add the cup of soaked mung dahl to boiling water in a pan so that the water reaches the top of the grains. Cook until almost all the water is evaporated and add the coconut grating, cumin, green chili, turmeric, and the salt and mix well. Add the grated onion and mix again. Cover the pan and let it cook in low heat for about 5 minutes.

In another pan heat the oil (3 tbsp.) and add the sliced onion. Fry until golden brown. Add the mung dahl mixture and mix well. Add salt to taste and mix well. Serve with rice.

CHICK-PEA CURRY

Ingredients

1 cup chick peas previously soaked overnight.

3 tomatoes sliced thick.

1 green pepper finely chopped.

2 tablespoons vegetable oil.

1 large onion sliced.

1 ½ teaspoon salt.

3 cloves of garlic.

½ teaspoon cayenne pepper.

½ teaspoon turmeric.

Pinch of black pepper.

Pinch of cinnamon and cloves.

¼ teaspoon cumin.

1 tablespoon lemon juice.

Preparation: Heat the vegetable oil in a pan and fry the onion. Add garlic, green pepper, cayenne and turmeric powder and fry for another 2 minutes. Add the tomatoes, cinnamon, salt, cloves, cumin, and the black pepper and cook for another 5 minutes. Add the chick-peas and the liquid which it was soaked in (about ½ cup) and cook on low heat for about half an hour. Stir in the lemon juice and the Chick-Pea Curry is ready to be served with rice.

MIXED VEGETABLE SALAD

Ingredients

1 large lettuce washed and cut.

Salt.

Several small radishes washed and sliced or whole.

Black pepper (ground)

4 tablespoons fresh lemon or lime juice.

3 medium tomatoes washed and sliced.

2 sliced tomatoes.

2 sliced carrots.

Tabasco sauce or red chili powder (½ tsp.)

2 lemons.

Preparation: In a large bowl mix the sliced lettuce together with the slices of onion. Add the salt and pepper. add 4 tablespoonfuls of fresh lemon or lime juice and mix well. Add the Tabasco sauce or the chili powder to desired taste. Arrange some of the sliced onion around the perimeter of a salad plate. Place the mixed lettuce in the center. Arrange the radishes, the sliced tomatoes and the sliced carrots on the salad. Cut the lemon into thin slices and arrange on the lettuce. Slice the tomato and arrange on top of the lettuce. Chill before serving.

MISCELLANEOUS PREPARATIONS

ROTI

Roti is a preparation made out of rice or wheat flour. The "bread" is similar to CHAPATIS and PARATHAS, a common Indian preparation, and PITA which is a Middle-Eastern preparation. Roti is usually substituted for rice to be consumed with several curries. Roti can be made plain or combined with certain ingredients for added taste.

PLAIN ROTI

Ingredients

2 cups of whole wheat flour or all-purpose flour.	½ teaspoon salt.
2 tablespoons vegetable oil or butter or margarine.	1 cup warm water.
½ cup shredded coconut.	½ cup coconut milk.

Preparation: Mix the wheat or all-purpose flour with the salt and the warm water in a bowl. Add the coconut milk and mix further until a firm dough is formed. Now add the shredded coconut and mix thoroughly. Add the oil and knead the dough until it is smooth and elastic. Separate the dough into several small sections and flatten each section into a thin rounded "pancake." Heat a skillet and smear with a little butter or oil so that the dough will not stick to the pan. (A nonstick pan will make the job easier.) Spread the pancake in the skillet or pan and allow to "cook" for about 30 seconds or until light brown.

Turn the roti over and cook the other side for about 30 seconds until brown. These rotis are then ready to be served with curries or with butter and jam spread on its surface.

SPICED ROTI

Preparation: Boil 2 medium sized potatoes. Remove the skin and cut into small sections. Slice a small onion into very thin slices. Heat 2 tablespoons of oil in a pan and add the onion and heat until brown. Add ½ teaspoon of curry paste or powder and mix well. Add the potato sections and a pinch of salt to taste and cook further for about 10 minutes. Make the dough as for plain roti. Add the potato mixture and mix thoroughly. Separate into smaller sections and cook as in the preparation of plain roti.

WATALAPPAN (PUDDING)

Watalappan is a common pudding somewhat similar to Western pudding.

Ingredients

1 cup coconut milk (This may Be made from hredded coconut or from coconut milk sold in canned form.)

8 eggs beaten up.

½ cup brown sugar or jaggery. (made from the coconut palm, available in Indian stores.)

3 tablespoons brown raisins.

Nutmeg – powder or shredded form (a pinch only).

Preparation: Add the sugar to the beaten up eggs and mix thoroughly. Add the coconut milk and the nutmeg and the raisins. Mix well again. Place the mixture in a bowl and over with a cloth. Steam the contents in the bowl in a steamer until the pudding becomes firm. A well prepared pudding should show spaces filled with syrup on the cut section.

Alternatively the mixture could be baked in the oven at 350º for 1 hour.

DESSERTS

Fresh fruits are by far the most common desserts or "after eats" as they are generally referred to in Sri Lanka. The following fruits are commonly found in Sri Lanka and are of very high nutrient value, particularly the vitamins.

MANGOES	PASSION FRUIT
PINEAPPLE	PAPAYA FRUIT
AVOCADO	GUAVA (PERA)
RIPE JACK FRUIT (WARAKA, WALA)	BANANAS (PLAINTAINS)

There are over 20 varieties. These fruits may be consumed alone when ripe or mixed together in the form of a fruit salad. When making a fruit salad the cut fruits are mixed together in a bowl and a small amount of condensed milk added. Sugar may be added for taste but is usually unnecessary as the ripe fruits are rich in different forms of sugar. The mixture should be chilled before being served.

SRI-LANKAN TEA

Sri Lanka grows the best tea in the world. Tea was introduced to CEYLON by the British during their reign until 1948 when Ceylon became an independent country. Tea is grown in the hills of Sri Lanka and is a major export of the country. Gourmet sections of most supermarkets and department stores carry Sri-Lankan tea (CEYLON TEA).

Preparation: Boil water in a tea kettle. Add 1 teaspoonful of Sri-Lankan tea for each person into a teapot and 1 for the pot! Let it stand covered for 5 minutes. Strain the tea into cups so the tea leaves are left behind. Some people may like to add a pinch of lemon while others like to adulterate the tea with a little milk and sugar. Remember though, tea has as much caffeine as does coffee!

CONCLUSION

It is possible that at first you may not like the strong aroma and the taste of curried food. But do not give up! The taste and aroma will grow on you and in time by practice you will learn to add the correct amount of each spice or the curry powder or the paste.

This little booklet is meant only to get you started in Sri-Lankan cooking. Once you learn the basics the possibilities are endless as you curry almost any kind of food.

I hope you enjoy the pleasures of SRI-LANKAN cuisine.

Printed in Great Britain
by Amazon.co.uk, Ltd.,
Marston Gate.